DISCARD

ALICE GUSTAFSON
SCHOOL
LEARNING CENTER

DATE DUE			

796.332   Karras, Steven
KAR   New York Giants
c. 1 $19.00   10-2017

D1294696

796.332
KAR
c.1

My First NFL Book

NEW YORK GIANTS

ALICE GUSTAFSON
SCHOOL
LEARNING CENTER

Steven M. Karras

LET'S READ
AV2 BY WEIGL
ADDED VALUE • AUDIO VISUAL

www.av2books.com

LET'S READ
AV²
BY WEIGL™
ADDED VALUE • AUDIO VISUAL

Go to **www.av2books.com**, and enter this book's unique code.

BOOK CODE

C 9 2 8 5 7 7

AV² by Weigl brings you media enhanced books that support active learning.

AV² provides enriched content that supplements and complements this book. Weigl's AV² books strive to create inspired learning and engage young minds in a total learning experience.

Your AV² Media Enhanced books come alive with...

Audio
Listen to sections of the book read aloud.

Video
Watch informative video clips.

Embedded Weblinks
Gain additional information for research.

Try This!
Complete activities and hands-on experiments.

Key Words
Study vocabulary, and complete a matching word activity.

Quizzes
Test your knowledge.

Slide Show
View images and captions, and prepare a presentation.

... and much, much more!

Published by AV² by Weigl
350 5th Avenue, 59th Floor
New York, NY 10118

Website: www.av2books.com

Copyright ©2018 AV² by Weigl
All rights reserved. No part of this publication may be reproduced, stored in a retrieval system, or transmitted in any form or by any means, electronic, mechanical, photocopying, recording, or otherwise, without the prior written permission of the publisher.

Library of Congress Control Number: 2017930782

ISBN 978-1-4896-5532-5 (hardcover)
ISBN 978-1-4896-5534-9 (multi-user eBook)

Printed in the United States of America in Brainerd, Minnesota
1 2 3 4 5 6 7 8 9 0 21 20 19 18 17

032017
020317

Editor: Katie Gillespie
Art Director: Terry Paulhus

Weigl acknowledges Getty Images and iStock as the primary image suppliers for this title.

NEW YORK GIANTS

CONTENTS

Team History

The New York Giants joined the NFL in 1925. They were one of the first five teams in the league. The team won 11 out of 13 games in 1927. They also won their first championship that year. The Giants played their first home games at the Polo Grounds in New York City.

Steve Owen was a Giants player who became the head coach for 23 seasons.

4

5

METLIFE STADIU

The Stadium

MetLife Stadium is the Giants' home field. It is the second largest stadium in the NFL. MetLife Stadium can hold up to 82,500 people. The New York Jets also play here. The painted grass in the endzones is on trays so it can be changed easily.

MetLife Stadium is in East Rutherford, New Jersey. It is a 20-minute train ride from New York City.

7

Team Spirit

Giants fans show a lot of spirit during games. Many have cheered on the team for years. The fans called the team's defense the "Big Blue Wrecking Crew" in the 1980s. The entire Giants team is now sometimes called "Big Blue."

Some fans show their spirit at games by painting the team colors on their faces.

8

9

The Jerseys

The Giants' jerseys changed between blue, red, and white for their first 28 years. Their home jerseys have stayed blue with white numbers since 1954. There is a small Giants logo on the front above the jersey number. The pants are gray with three stripes.

The Helmet

The Giants' helmets are blue with a red stripe down the center. The team's logo is a lowercase "ny" for New York. The logo is on both sides of the helmet. Each player's number is in big white numbers on both the front and back of the helmet.

Plastic helmets were first used in the 1940s.

The Coach

Ben McAdoo is the Giants' head coach. McAdoo was hired for this job in 2016. He coached the Giants' offense for two years before that. The Giants had the eighth best offense in the NFL during that time. McAdoo was an assistant coach for the Green Bay Packers before he worked for the Giants.

ALICE GUSTAFSON
SCHOOL
LEARNING CENTER

15

Player Positions

Guards on the offense protect their quarterback from being tackled. They also block the defense so running backs can run with the ball. There are two guards in the offense. Guards are some of the biggest players on the field.

Blocking is how the offense stops the defense from tackling the player with the ball.

16

Star Player

Eli Manning is the Giants' quarterback. He holds the team record for most completed passes. He has thrown 309 touchdown passes in 13 seasons. This is also a team record. Manning was named the NFL's Most Valuable Player in 2008 and 2012. His father and brother also played in the NFL.

was
a running back for the
Giants. He led the team
to the NFL championship
in 1956. He was also
voted Player of the
Year that year. Gifford
scored 78 touchdowns.
This is the most in team
history. He also threw
14 touchdowns. Gifford
was added to the Pro
Football Hall of Fame
in 1977.

Famous Player

Team Records

The Giants have won four NFL championships and four Super Bowls. One famous Giants player was Mel Hein. Hein was on the Giants' offense for a team record of 15 seasons. Tiki Barber had 10,499 rushing yards with the Giants. This is a team record.

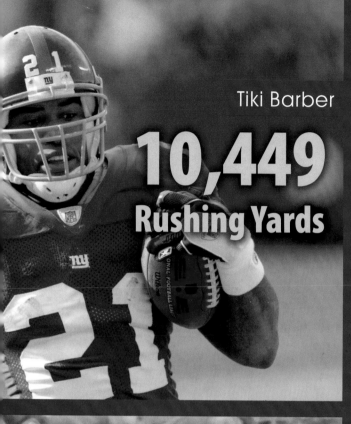

Tiki Barber

10,449
Rushing Yards

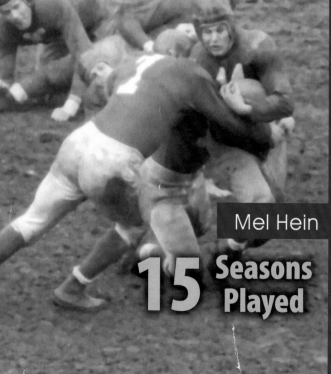

Mel Hein

15 **Seasons**
Played

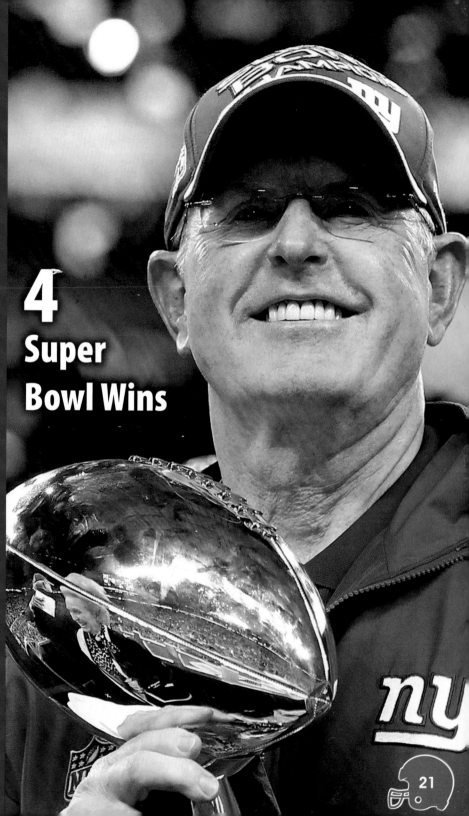

4
Super
Bowl Wins

21

By the Numbers

Quarterback Y. A. Tittle set a team record of **36** touchdown passes in one season.

Defensive end Michael Strahan played in a record **216** regular season games.

The **#14** jersey has been retired twice.

Giants founder Tim Mara paid $500 to start the team in 1925.

MetLife Stadium cost $1.6 billion to build.

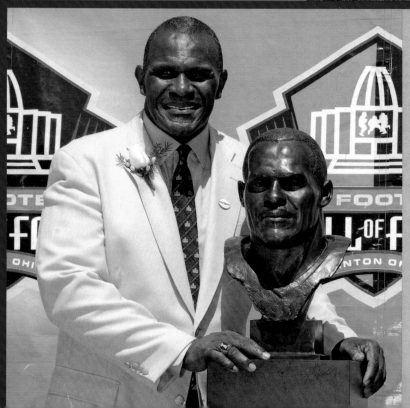

28 New York Giants are in the Pro Football Hall of Fame.

Quiz

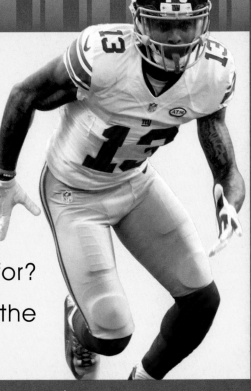

1. In which year did the Giants win their first championship?

2. How many people can MetLife Stadium hold?

3. What was the Giants' defense called in the 1980s?

4. What does the team's logo stand for?

5. When was Frank Gifford added to the Pro Football Hall of Fame?

ANSWERS 1. 1927 2. Up to 82,500 3. "Big Blue Wrecking Crew" 4. New York 5. 1977

MEDIA ENHANCED BOOKS
AV2 BY WEIGL™
ADDED VALUE • AUDIO VISUAL

Check out www.av2books.com for activities, videos, audio clips, and more!

The AV² Collection

1 Go to www.av2books.com.

2 Enter book code. | C 9 2 8 5 7 7 |

3 Fuel your imagination online!

www.av2books.com